For everyone, and everything, who loves to dance.
—RR

To João - keep dancing!
—HA

Text © 2023 by Rekha S. Rajan
Illustrations © 2023 by Hannah Abbo
Cover and internal design © 2023 by Sourcebooks
Sourcebooks and the colophon are registered trademarks of Sourcebooks.
All rights reserved.
The characters and events portrayed in this book are fictitious or are used fictitiously.
Any similarity to real persons, living or dead, is purely coincidental and not intended by the author.
The full color art was created using a mixture of gouache paint and colored pencils, then finished on a tablet with digital illustrations and scanned textures.
Published by Sourcebooks eXplore, an imprint of Sourcebooks Kids
P.O. Box 4410, Naperville, Illinois 60567-4410
(630) 961-3900
sourcebookskids.com
Cataloging-in-Publication Data is on file with the Library of Congress.
Source of Production: Wing King Tong Paper Products Co. Ltd., Shenzhen, Guangdong Province, China
Date of Production: February 2023
Run Number: 5029734
Printed and bound in China.
WKT 10 9 8 7 6 5 4 3 2 1

Can you Dance Like A Peacock?

Words by
Rekha S. Rajan

Pictures by
Hannah Abbo

sourcebooks
eXplore

Raise your hand if you love to dance!

People LOVE to dance!

On the streets, in classrooms, on stage, and with our families at home.

But did you know that animals also love to dance?

LOOK at this beautiful **PEACOCK**.

He is so proud of his long neck and wants to show off his

blue, green, and purple feathers

as they flutter in the wind.

He stretches his neck up when he takes a big step to
STRUT STRUT STRUT!

Peacocks LOVE to dance!

Across the road
and through the field,
waving their vibrant tails in the wind to make new friends.

DANCE BREAK!

Can **YOU** dance like a peacock?

Stand up straight,   fluff your feathers,   stretch your neck and

STRUT! STRUT! STRUT!

There's another animal who loves to dance!

The tall, striped **GAZELLE**

shakes his long head, and sharp, curved antlers from side to side.

He stops when he hears a rustling from behind a bush.

The gazelle arches his back and

leaps into the air with all four legs to

STOT! STOT! STOT!

Gazelles LOVE to dance!

When a predator comes close,
gazelles leap through stalks of tall,
green grass to warn their family of DANGER.

DANCE BREAK!

Can **YOU** dance like a gazelle?

Bend your knees,

leap into the air, and

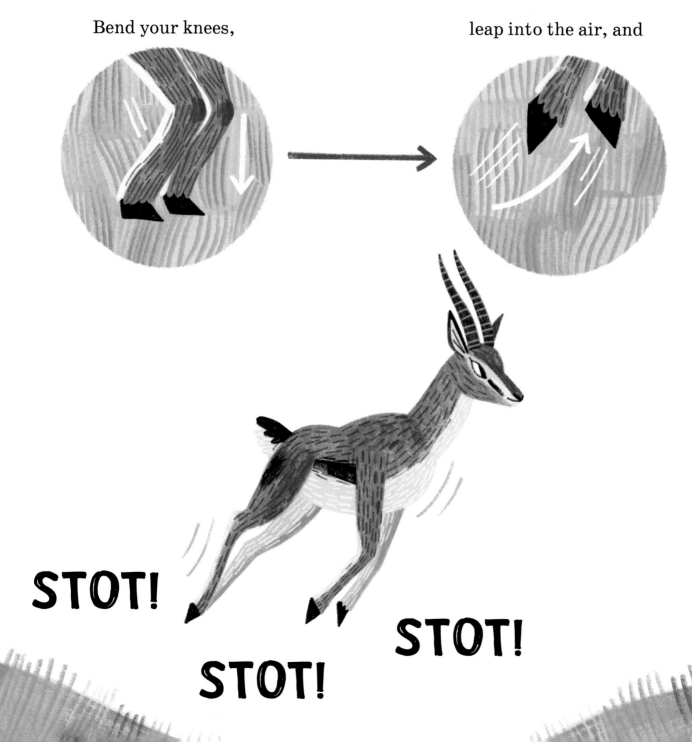

STOT!

STOT!

STOT!

DO YOU HEAR THAT?

Bzzzzzzzzzzzzz

As hundreds and hundreds of black-and-yellow **HONEYBEES**

swirl across the honeycomb,

they shake their hips

front and back and

WAGGLE! WAGGLE! WAGGLE!

Honeybees LOVE to dance!

When they find the tallest, biggest flowers in the garden,
they rush back to the hive to dance for their brothers and sisters
and cousins, to show how to
get
that
honey!

DANCE BREAK!

Can **YOU** dance like a honeybee?

Put your hands on your hips

and buzz around the room as you

WAGGLE! WAGGLE! WAGGLE!

SPLASH!

In the swirling, swishing tides,
the **DOLPHIN** flips her tail

arches her back,

points her nose up

and jumps out of the ocean!

Dolphins LOVE to dance

as they leap, and dive, and twist, and spin

to exercise and feel energized.

DANCE BREAK!

Can **YOU** dance like a dolphin?

Put your arms straight up,   hands together,   and jump high to

SPLASH! SPLASH! SPLASH!

DOWN THERE! Next to that rock!
The **DUNG BEETLE** rolls his food into a big, round ball
to take back home for a tasty meal.

He stands on top and turns
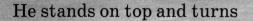
the way
all around.

The dung beetle LOVES to dance

as he protects his lunch (a crunchy ball of poop) from other beetles.

DANCE BREAK!

Can **YOU** dance like the dung beetle?

Put your arms out to the side, find your space, and

TURN! TURN! TURN!

SHHHHHH!!!

Deep in the ocean is the **SPANISH DANCER SEA SLUG**

who is sleeping in a small, dark cave.

If you wake her up,

she opens her bright, red tentacles to

CHA CHA CHA

and scurry away to safety.

The Spanish dancer sea slug LOVES to dance.

When there is danger, she uses the moving waters to dance and glide away to safety.

DANCE BREAK!

Can **YOU** dance like the Spanish dancer sea slug?

Get down low and

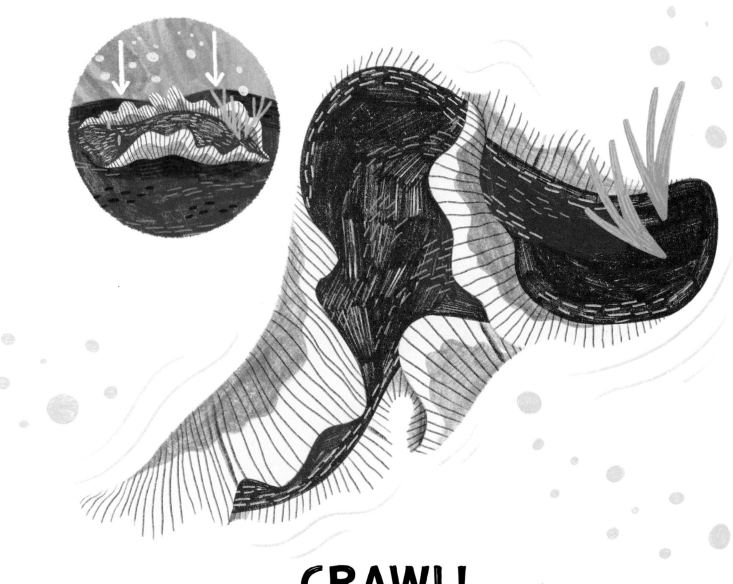

CRAWL! CRAWL! CRAWL!

LOOK at all that pink, pink, PINK!
The **FLAMINGOS** dance in a group,

stepping together through shallow waters,
looking for someone to love as they

MARCH!

MARCH!

MARCH!

Flamingos LOVE to dance.

They step, step, step,

turn, turn, turn,

and march, march, march across the shallow waters.

DANCE BREAK!

Find a partner,

stand close together, and

MARCH!

MARCH!

MARCH!

Animals have different ways of dancing that make them unique!

They strut and stot and
waggle and splash.

They turn and crawl

and march, march, march!

But there is one dance
that is the best dance of all.

It's the dance moves
that are inside of you!

Now stand up and show how
YOU dance!

DYNAMIC DANCERS

THE PEACOCK DANCE

The peacock is the name for the male species of the peafowl. Only the male peacocks have long, beautiful feathers. The female is called a peahen. The baby is called a peachick. When the male peacocks are looking for a female friend, they open their tails into a fan and slowly turn in a circle to make sure that everyone can see them! Look at the feathers. The center is called the "eye." The open tail of feathers fanning the back of the peacock is called a train.

Peacocks often dance before it rains. Peacocks are native to a region in India and South Asia where monsoon—heavy rain—season occurs at the same time of year they're looking for a mate. Some scientists call this the peacock rain dance. The raindrops make their feathers glisten like diamonds!

THE GAZELLE DANCE

The gazelle is part of the antelope family. Unlike other animals in this family, both male and female gazelles have horns! The word "stot" means to bounce or jump or spring up into the air on all four legs! Many farm animals stot. Lambs and goats stot across the farm to play and get exercise. It looks like they are bouncing on a trampoline.

When the gazelle stots, it is showing the predators in the African plains that they are fast and quick. It is saying, "You can't catch me!"

THE HONEYBEE WAGGLE DANCE

Honeybees are hardworking insects who work together in a colony. When bees find a great source of pollen or nectar, they quickly rush back to the hive.

But bees can't talk! They use their bodies to dance and show their family and friends where to find the best pollen or nectar. Honeybees look at the flower and then they look at the sun. The honeybees then fly in the opposite direction of the sun to create an angle for other bees to follow.

Honeybees are always looking for new places to find food. When they find a new food source, they start to waggle, waggle, waggle and dance. The waggle dance is when honeybees use their hips and bodies to point to the direction of where to find food! Sometimes, it even looks like a figure eight.

THE DOLPHIN DANCE

Dolphins are very social animals. They love to swim and splash together! When dolphins dance and flip in the ocean, it looks like they are doing tricks or performing a show. But their dances are not choreographed—that means they didn't practice their moves! Swimming through the ocean is hard work, so dolphins leap over the waves to conserve (or save) their energy.

Dolphins dance to communicate with each other and to find a quick way to travel through the wide ocean. When they dance and perform shows at aquariums and water parks, these are natural behaviors they would do in the wild. Dolphins love an audience. If you see them dancing, give them a big round of applause!

THE DUNG BEETLE DANCE

The dung beetle has to search for food every day. It looks for big piles of dung and then scrapes out a piece that looks tasty. When it rolls its food into a ball, it's also dancing backwards! The dung beetle cannot see if other beetles might be coming for this tasty snack. So, it turns, turns, turns around, 360 degrees, and rolls the ball to a safe place.

When the dung beetle is ready for dinner, it finds a big, round, ball of poop and climbs on top. Scientists call this the dung beetle dance. Don't have dinner with a dung beetle! It does not like company. When the dung beetle dances, it is saying, "This food is mine!"

THE SPANISH DANCER SEA SLUG DANCE

The Spanish dancer sea slug is part of a family called a *nudibranch*—or mollusk. That means they shed their shell when they are babies. It is also the largest type of mollusk. The Spanish dancer sea slug spends the day crawling along the sandy ocean floor.

The Spanish dancer sea slug got its name because scientists thought its movements were like Spanish flamenco dancers who twirl their beautiful, red dresses on stage! The bright red, orange, and yellow colors of this creature warn predators, "I am poisonous! Don't eat me!"

THE FLAMINGO DANCE

Flamingos are famous for their bright pink color. But they are actually born with fuzzy, white fur. They get their coloring from the food they eat! The vitamin called beta-carotene has a natural pigmentation (a dye or coloring) that is pink and red and orange. This is the same vitamin found in carrots and beets and pumpkins. When flamingos are ready to find love, they dance together in a parade. The flamingos dance as they turn to the right, turn to the left, and repeat this pattern in a group.

A group of flamingos dancing will definitely make you stand up and look! This grouping is called a flamboyance. The word flamboyance means colorful, bright, and attractive.

KIDS IN MOTION (For teachers and parents)

The national standards for early childhood and elementary physical education include five benchmarks: movement skills, rules and safety, team-building, principles of health promotion and prevention, and human body systems. Movement is an important part of a young child's education and physical development.

Activity—Understanding Movement

While the animals and insects are not taught how to move their bodies to communicate and survive, it is important for young children to learn how to move in a safe space, be respectful of others, and gain control of their large muscles through hopping, standing, turning, and crawling. During each dance break, ask children what parts of their bodies are being used to move and dance. Discuss how it feels to jump up and down on both legs or stot (jump on all fours like the gazelle), why you have to be careful when turning like a peacock or dung beetle, and how it feels different to move fast like the honeybees or slow and graceful like the sea slug.

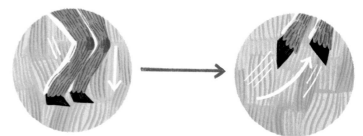

Activity—Graphing Groups

In this book, children are introduced to how animals and insects move their bodies to find friends, collect food, and exercise! Some of the creatures move and dance alone while others work in pairs or a large group. Have children categorize the animals by their choice of dancing alone or with others on a piece of paper or as a large group in class. Follow up by asking children if they prefer to dance alone, with a partner, or in a group.

This activity can also be expanded to graph and categorize why the animals move and dance. Some categories can include: to find a mate/friend, collect food, hide, find protection, warn others, and exercise.

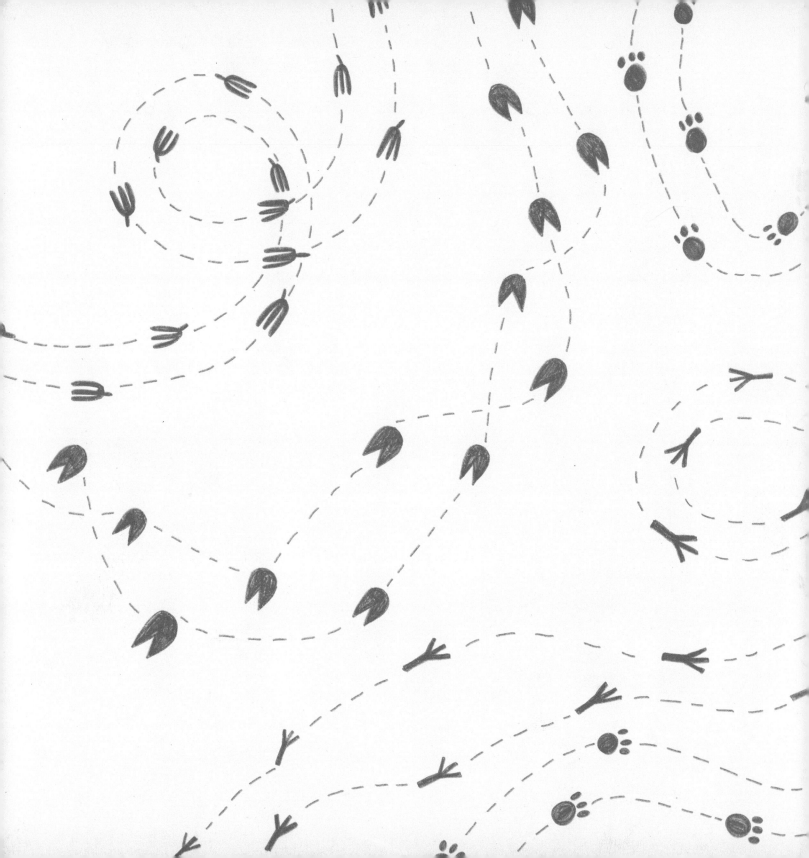